Above:
Where the soaring cliffs of Taiaroa Head (Pukekura) meet the open ocean – a colourful and spectacular place.

Left:
Central city symmetry: Moray Place encircles the Octagon, with the Town Hall in the foreground and the harbour basin in the distance.

FRONT COVER
The Dunedin Railway Station, built of basalt and limestone, was completed in 1906. It remains New Zealand's grandest railway station. Restoration work was undertaken in 1998.
Inset top: Larnach Castle, Otago Peninsula
Inset bottom: The bronze statue of Scottish poet Robert Burns has pride of place in the Octagon, opposite St Paul's Cathedral.

Inside front cover
Larnach Castle has a lofty position on Otago Peninsula, overlooking Otago Harbour. Portobello and Harwood are in the distance.

Photography and text by Neville Peat

Range), giving a total population of 120,000 and an extraordinarily large land area – 3350 square kilometres. Farms, country towns and bright, shiny city shopping malls are all part of Dunedin.

The city enjoys a temperate climate thanks largely to its coastal location. Rainfall and sunshine come in fair measure, but at this latitude (46 degrees south) changes in the weather can be dramatic. Cool, moist south-west fronts alternate with warm, dry northerlies or the vigorous north-easterlies that drape carpets of fluffy cloud on the summit of Mount Cargill. One thing is for sure – the weather is never monotonous.

Dunedin's name is a Gaelic form of Edinburgh, from which city Dunedin has acquired many of its street names. 'Edinburgh of the South' is how the city is sometimes described, although to those who love the physical setting, the convivial, traditional feel and the many natural and recreational features of the place, Dunedin might more aptly be called 'Eden of the South'.

PANORAMIC SETTING . . .

Dunedin's landscape is dominated by an extensive set of volcanic hills. The volcano that created them 10 million years ago is long dormant but subsequent erosion has produced a cradle for both city and harbour. Panoramas abound, and at various lookouts that can be reached by car there are bronze, circular tables indicating the sweep of landmarks within view. There is one such table on Mount Cargill, 680 metres above sea level.

Otago Peninsula is a visual treat, tied to the mainland by a flat sandy strip and indented on the ocean side by two large inlets. Most of the settlement is on the harbour side; high, surf-beaten bluffs and lonely beaches characterise the ocean coast, the domain of seals and sea birds.

Inland, Dunedin City stretches beyond the Taieri Gorge to the Rock and Pillar Range, easternmost of Central Otago's great ranges.

Left:
Otago Harbour, in the vicinity of Port Chalmers, and the peninsula beyond – a view from the top of Mount Cargill.

Right:
View east from Mount Cargill: Sawyers Bay, harbour islands and Papanui Inlet in the distance.

Lower left:
The Octagon, pivot of the city, in midsummer.

Below:
Snow tussock on the brow of Flagstaff, overlooking the city.

The heart of tertiary education in Dunedin – Otago University's campus in the foreground, with Otago Polytechnic and the College of Education beyond, adjacent to Logan Park. Dunedin's modest river, the Water of Leith, meanders through it all.

Port Chalmers basking in afternoon sun, with Portobello and Harbour Cone in the distance.

Giant container ships are frequent visitors to Port Chalmers.

The *Monarch* passing the islands in the middle of the harbour on one of her cruises. Harbour Cone is in the distance.

Not the Greek Isles, but Taiaroa Head, also known as Pukekura, destination for harbour cruises. The lighthouse marks the entrance to Otago Harbour.

Careys Bay, near Port Chalmers, is a haven for fishing boats and yachts.

Left:
This autumn look to Logan Park Drive is deceptive – the North American poplars are wearing new spring growth.

Right:
Weathered and wave-worn sandstone cliffs, Tunnel Beach.

Left:
Dalmore houses and the snow-laden slopes of Flagstaff shine under winter sun.

Right:
A painted boat upon a painted shore at Aramoana.

Above:
Lovers Leap, on Otago Peninsula, is a breathtaking eroded sea cliff and rock arch, 224 metres from top to bottom.

Left:
A crescent of creamy sand marks the city beaches of St Clair (foreground) and St Kilda.

Lower left:
Sandfly Bay, Otago Peninsula . . . alluringly wild.

Below:
Sandfly Bay surf wears a mane of spray, complementing the lion's head profile of the adjacent island.

Above:
Campus area, University of Otago.

Above right:
The Taieri Gorge, in Dunedin's hinterland, is a feature attraction of a regular tourist train trip. Here the train emerges from a tunnel to cross the Taieri River at Hindon.

Left:
A small river, the Water of Leith, is well channelled as it flows through the university grounds.

Right:
The Strath Taieri valley is the tourist train's destination. Near Middlemarch, at Dunedin's western boundary, is the striking hill called Smooth Cone and this abandoned stone cottage.

NATURALLY . . .

From the rocks up, Dunedin is a natural treasure trove – animal, vegetable and mineral.

The spectacular geology includes stacks of black basalt columns and smooth sandstone cliffs. The vegetation ranges from salt marsh at sea level to sub-alpine communities, including snow tussock grasses, on the hilltops, with patches of tall native forest (rimu, totara and cedar) at intermediate altitudes, notably on the flanks of Mount Cargill. Closer to the city centre is a decorative ribbon of native and exotic trees called the Town Belt that extends for over 4 kilometres.

Above all, though, Dunedin is known as the natural history capital of New Zealand because of its wildlife – its albatrosses, penguins, seals and shags (cormorants). Royal albatrosses, among the largest of all sea birds, have chosen to nest at Taiaroa Head on the tip of Otago Peninsula – the only mainland colony in the world. The peninsula is the main breeding area on mainland New Zealand for yellow-eyed penguins (hoiho), and seals routinely haul out on the rocky headlands and beaches. A convenient place to see native land birds is the Botanic Gardens where tui, bellbirds, fantails and pigeons fly free and other species live in an aviary.

One of the biggest and grandest birds of all, the royal albatross, makes its home at Taiaroa Head. Chicks are raised by breeding pairs every second year. In their off-year the birds roam the great Southern Ocean. Their wingspan averages 3 metres. *Greg Gordon photos*

Left:
This yellow-eyed penguin, fresh from a day's fishing offshore, waddles home to its nest in flax or scrub on an Otago Peninsula beach.

Far left:
Yellow-eyed penguins running ashore at dusk, Otago Peninsula.

The Pyramids, Otago Peninsula, are wave-worn mounds of volcanic rock, 20 minutes' easy walk from a road end.

Far right:
An impressive outcrop of rock columns is the Organ Pipes formation on the slopes of Mount Cargill.

Dunedin's climate is considered one of the best for cultivating rhododendrons. There are about 2000 varieties at the Botanic Gardens.

Far right::
Basalt rock columns, stacked on their side or tilted, form one of the wave-worn Pyramids on Otago Peninsula. A cave underlies this pyramid.

Below:
In spring, the Botanic Gardens' rockery is a riot of colour.

A family of
white-fronted terns,
Aramoana.

Lower left:
In spring, when the
kowhai blooms
around Dunedin,
silvereyes and other
nectar-loving native
bush birds are in their
element.

Below:
Native pigeon
numbers are
increasing around
Dunedin's leafy
suburbs. This one is
perched in a manuka
tree at Bethunes
Gully.

Mature native forest
decorates the slopes
of the Leith Valley
near its saddle. The
trees with conical
crowns are native
cedar.

From a height of 1000 metres this is how the city, harbour and Otago Peninsula appear on a strikingly fine day. *Perran Tonkin photo*

Dunedin's showpiece stately home, Olveston, was built in 1904–06 for a businessman, David Theomin, who furnished and decorated it in grand style. It was bequeathed to the city by his daughter, Dorothy, in 1966.

Olveston's grand hall. The oak staircase, which contains no nails, was shipped out from Britain.

At Glenfalloch, this kauri homestead, built last century, stands in a magnificent woodland garden that is open to the public.

GRANDEUR AND TRADITION . . .

Dunedin is a showpiece city for Victorian and Edwardian architecture, lovely old buildings that, in the main, have escaped the northern rush to mirror glass and bland design. Stone spires still dominate the skyline. Volcanic stone and Oamaru stone (a form of limestone) are to be seen everywhere in public buildings, business houses and private residences. Rock-solid is this city.

Architectural diversity is a feature, with timber and brick supplementing stone as a building medium. But stone towers and ramparts create the most lasting impression – First Church, St Pauls, the Municipal Chambers, Larnach Castle, the university clocktower, Otago Boys High, the Railway Station and so on.

The Scottish settlers' emphasis on education shows through not only in the tertiary institutions but also in the city's libraries and museums, with Otago Museum featuring a magnificent Maori hall and natural history displays.

Above right:
Dunedin has New Zealand's only whisky distillery, Wilsons.

Right:
The Scottish Shop in George Street reflects the city's origins.

Below:
Taste of Scotland: haggis ceremonies are performed on request in Dunedin, complete with bagpipe music, knife-wielding ritual and the recitation of Robert Burns' famous verse to the 'Great chieftain o' the puddin' race'. Whisky, made in Dunedin, is a necessary accompaniment. *Lindsay McLeod photo*

Spring in the Octagon:
daffodils add charm to
a fine spring morning
below Robbie Burns'
statue and the
Municipal Chambers.

Above:
Dunedin Railway Station is New Zealand's most splendid, built of basalt and limestone and completed in 1906. It earned its designer, George Troup, a knighthood.

Right:
Stained glass window, Railway Station.

Below:
Steam relic: a JA 482 steam locomotive, one of the last of its type, retired from service in 1971, stands polished and proud in a glass display case beside the Otago Settlers' Museum.

Above:
Portraits of Otago's European pioneers look down on an ornate 19th-century bank desk in a feature gallery in the Otago Settlers' Museum.

Above right:
Old-timer: Josephine, a Fairlie double-boiler, double-bogie locomotive that first saw service in 1872, is a popular exhibit at the museum.

Right:
'Thread of Life' is the name given to this bronze figure at the Centennial Memorial (1840–1940) on Signal Hill.

Opposite page:
Foothold of Presbyterianism: First Church of Otago stands on Bell Hill in central Dunedin. Opened in 1873, it took six years to build. The spire is 56 metres high.

Right:
These tall semi-detached houses on the university campus were completed in 1879 for the families of the first professors. Today they house the Music Department and University Extension. They were roughcast with orange Moeraki gravel in 1957.

Below:
This large residence, Linden, in Royal Terrace was built of brick and plaster in 1878 and later occupied by Richard Hudson, who founded a chocolate and biscuit factory now incorporated in Cadbury Confectionery Ltd.

Above right:
Elegant student accommodation – Studholme Hall, Clyde Street.

Right:
This 19th-century wooden cottage in Haywood Street features a steeply pitched roof and diagonal weatherboarding. An early pre-fab, sent out from Britain, it dates from the late 1850s. The timber in it is mainly Baltic pine.

Above and lower left:
The university
clocktower and
registry building
occupy a picturesque
setting beside the
Leith.

Left:
Landmark of tertiary
education: the
university clocktower.

Right:
Industrial architecture of another era: this old flour mill, built for the Crown company, dates from 1867. The top two floors were added in 1890 and steel rolling equipment was then installed.

Below:
Bay-window terrace houses in Stuart Street, now used mainly as shops, offices and restaurants.

Left:
St Pauls, Dunedin's Anglican Cathedral, strikes a Gothic profile in the Octagon. It was built of Oamaru stone in 1915–19, replacing the first St Pauls, which was consecrated on the same site in 1863.

Below:
The stone turrets of Otago Boys High School are well known to generations of Dunedin schoolboys.

The Fortune, Dunedin's only professional theatre, occupies a remodelled old stone church in Moray Place.

Chingford Stables, built of volcanic bluestone in 1880, used to house the Arab stallions of a leading city businessman. Today, surrounded by magnificent trees, including a massive macrocarpa, the building is used for public and private functions.

The 23-metre-high valve tower at the Ross Creek Reservoir, completed in 1867, is the oldest structure of its kind still standing in New Zealand.

Upper:
The church at Otakou Marae was built to mark the 1940 centenary of the Treaty of Waitangi signing. Several chiefs who signed the treaty are buried in the urupa behind the church.

Above left:
Otago Museum is renowned for its Maori gallery, which includes this reconstruction of a moa-hunter camp near the mouth of the Shag River.

Above right:
This stone, with a mysterious spiral carving on its upper surface, was found on the seashore at Cape Egmont, Taranaki, and transferred to Dunedin in 1988 as a memorial to the Maori prisoners from that province who were kept at Dunedin last century.

AT PLAY . . .

Dunedin's harbour, ocean beaches and hilly topography provide a ready-made setting for all kinds of recreation. To complete the picture, lake (Waihola) and river (Taieri) are half an hour's drive from the city, on the Taieri Plain.

Organised sports events utilise such venues as Carisbrook and Logan Parks, the Dunedin Stadium and Moana Pool, but there is tremendous scope for informal recreation, from board sailing to mountain bike excursions and bush walks. To the fit and active, Dunedin can appear as one big playground.

Above:
Surf rafting (with motor) offers invigorating entertainment. White Island in the distance is a destination.
Left:
First dip: trying out the surf at St Clair.

Below:
Volleyball on St Clair beach.

Above:
Saturday sport – cricketers at Logan Park, board sailors on the harbour.

Left:
Rugby star Jeff Wilson, seen here playing for the All Blacks against England, is a favourite with the Carisbrook crowds.
Mark Reeves (photo)

One of the shortest and most impressive walks in the Dunedin area is to the sandstone cliffs of Tunnel Beach.

Baldwin Street, North-east Valley, is reputed to be the 'world's steepest street', concreted for vehicle traction. There is an annual race up and down the street – the Baldwin Street 'Gutbuster'. The record is around 2 minutes.

First published 1991
HYNDMAN PUBLISHING
P.O. BOX 5017
DUNEDIN

Reprinted 1992, 1993, 1994, 1995, 1996, 1997

Revised edition 1998, Reprinted 1999, 2000, 2001

ISBN 1 86934 031 0

Designed and printed through
Bookprint Consultants, Wellington

Inside back cover (upper):
Sunset surfer, Black Head.

Inside back cover (lower):
Harbour cone, a volcanic peak, looms over the harbour-side village of Portobello.